Love And Life

by

Sandra Grady

Love And Life

Copyright © 2001 by Sandra Grady

All rights reserved under International and Pan-American copyright conventions. No part of this book may be reproduced, stored in a retrieval system or transmitted in any form, electronic, mechanical, or by other means, without written permission of the author.

Library of Congress
Cataloging in Publication Data

ISBN 1-58235-919-9

Manufactured in The United States of America by
Watermark Press
6 Gwynns Mill Court
Owings Mills, MD 21117
410-654-0400

To my loving mother, Dorothy Grady whose courage, strength, and faith I truly admire. You are my best friend and I love you more than anyone in the world.

This book is also dedicated to the memory of:

My grandmother
My sister Sheila
My sister Serena
My brother Victor

Table of Contents

Preface
Introduction

Mother • 11

Fundamentals

Love • 14
Life • 15
Success • 16
Happiness • 17
Time • 18

From Detroit to Hollywood

I Came Out Here To Be A Star • 20

Relationships I've Known Or Known About

Michael • 25
Mark • 26
Sometimes I Want To Feel... • 28
No, You Can't Come Back • 29
You Had It All Lover • 31
Love Fantasy • 32
You Touched My Soul • 34
Rainbow Love • 35
You Gave Me Hope • 36

Yes, I'm Ready

Basics • 40
The Frame • 42
Women and Men • 43
Us • 44
Take My Hand • 45

Progression

Sea of Tranquility • 49
Hiding • 50
Flaunt It • 51

Mellowing

The Roses • 55
Joy • 56
Stop and Smell the Roses • 57
I Have the Power • 59

Food For Thought

The Rain • 62
Sometimes I Wonder... • 63

Preface

I believe that love is the most important thing in life. It colors who you are. It influences your personality, attitude, lifestyle, career, happiness and quality of life. Because love is so complex sometimes, we may find ourselves going through a myriad of emotions, both good and bad. The collection of works in this book expresses that.

I am truly blessed to be able to publish this book and I thank everyone who reads it.

Introduction

Love and Life is Sandra Grady's first book of poetry. However, she has had two poems published by the International Library of Poetry. In 1999, "Time" was printed in an anthology entitled *Serenity At Daybreak*. In 2000, "The Rain" was printed in an anthology entitled *Home At Last*. These poems are read around the world. This exposure has motivated Sandra to gather old and new works and present them in her own book. As her career evolved from model to actress to counselor, she continued to write when inspired. She is very proud of the fruits of her labor. Ms. Grady is also listed in the International Who's Who of Professionals 1999 edition.

Mother

Makes me feel special.
Only talks positive.
The most important person to me.
Heavenly spirit.
Everybody loves her.
Remembers and recognizes my birthday.

Fundamentals

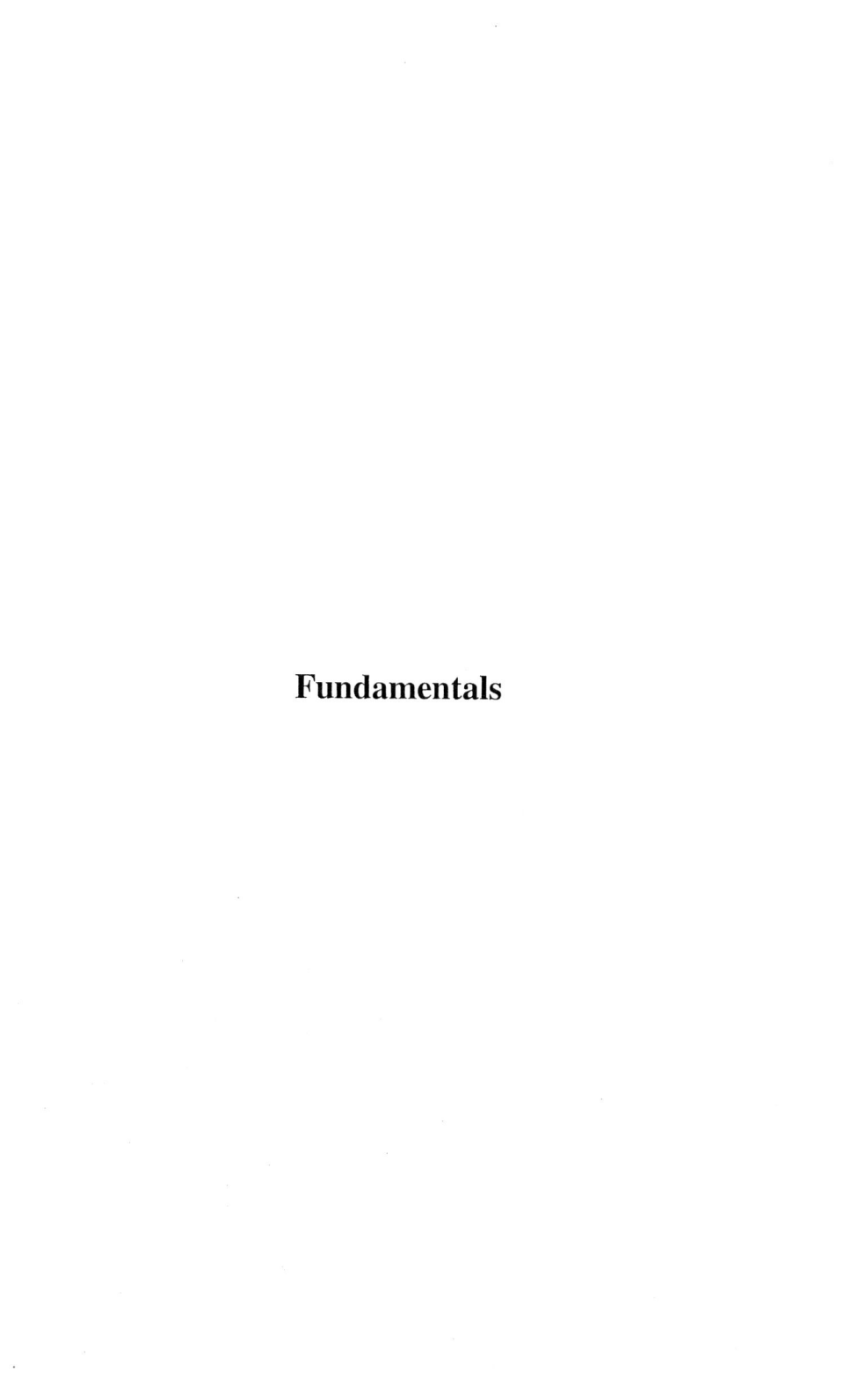

Love

Learning who you are.
Owning who you are.
Valuing yourself.
Eager to be the best that you can be.

Life

Love yourself and others.
Invest in yourself by fulfilling your potential and help others do the same.
Find yourself and your place in this world.
Enjoy the precious gift of life.

Success

<u>S</u>urvival of the fittest.
<u>U</u>nderstanding the scheme of life.
<u>C</u>aring about people more than money.
<u>C</u>apable of achieving goals.
<u>E</u>xercise good judgement.
<u>S</u>ure about yourself.
<u>S</u>et a positive example.

Happiness

Have a good time.
Always have a smile.
Please yourself and others.
Practice what you preach.
If life gives you lemons, make some lemonade.
Never give up on yourself.
Exercise your mind and your body.
Show love for yourself and others.
Set a positive example.

Time

It's time to love
Hate will only destroy
Time helps to heal
But it also brings losses
Temporary youth
And the realization
That our loved ones
Are only on loan to us
We need more time
But there is no more to be had
What have you done
With all your gifts
Didn't you know
They were perishable
If your life is filled with love
Time will be kind to you

From Detroit

To Hollywood

I Came Out Here To Be A Star

You oughta be in Hollywood
With your looks and talent
success will come easy
This city is too small for you
Go west young girl
Be your best
Take that screen test
Get a portfolio
Model that sassy sexy body
Show off those exotic eyes
and high cheek bones
A good agent will help you win the prize.

So I came out here to be a star
because they said that my looks and talent
would overwhelm.
With each day
I saw more and more like me.
It clearly won't be as easy
as one, two, three.

I got the agent, the pictures
and some parts.
But was not willing to
scratch anybody's back
to make the right connections.

You'll never make it out here
with those morals and values.
So decide what your priorities are
if you really want to be a star.
There are many beautiful girls like you
who are more than willing to do the do.
What will it be?
Do I need to set you free?

I came out here to be a star
and that is what I am.
To be true to my self
and not let Hollyweird change me
is quite a success.
Faith in myself
will take me very far.

Relationships I've Known

Or Known About

Michael

Out of nowhere you came
to enter my life
and bring a positive change
Your eyes were so true
and your heart just
shined through
with love and affection
as sweet as
the most exquisite confection
You are such a good man
because each day
you give me everything that you can
I've been waiting for so long
for that special someone
to enter my soul
and hear my love songs
Welcome Michael
and enjoy the music

Mark

Out of nowhere he came
to pay a visit to this dame.
Very businesslike I must say.
Didn't think I would see him after that day.
A question came up
so I gave him a call
Then he invited me
to a game of women's basketball.
Oh no! Not me.
The females don't strike my fancy.
Michael Jordan or someone like that
I would have said yes right off the bat.
His professional voice is gone now
when he asks me to take a vow
to call him about the vacant house across the street.
This scenario is getting more and more upbeat.
With his home number now in hand
I decided to call the man.
My professional voice was gone now
Because I wanted to see if he could make me say wow.

The business info was quickly given
Then he asked me to share some fun livin'.
We went out on a date
and it was so very great.
A self-described boring and simple man
Well, you now have a fan.
I sense your good heart
and it's obvious you're smart.
I enjoyed sharing your space
and looking at that very nice face.
Holding your hand was such a joy
I can't wait to see you again big boy.
Thank you Mark for being who you are
because being with you
makes me feel like a star.

Sometimes I Want To Feel...

Sometimes I want to feel
Feel the love that you say you have for me
We've had our ups and downs
and grown really closer together
I've seen you change from a boy to a man
And you helped guide me to womanhood
We know so much about each other
inside and out
A bond has been created
that can't be torn apart
We discovered that when we strayed away
and then returned to our roots
Our lives are intertwined
We are a part of one another
You say you love me
But there seems to be some reservation
I know where your heart is
but sometimes I want to feel
Feel the love that you say you have for me
Open up and let all your inhibitions go
We've come too far to hold back
Let it go
Make me feel it
I know its there
But I've got to really feel it
I won't leave again
Sometimes I want to feel
Feel the love that you say you have for me.

No, You Can't Come Back

Time has passed
since you said good-bye.
You thought the grass would be greener,
so you gave it a try.

We always want something that doesn't exist
and the reality hits us after the kiss.
So now you realize that I was the best.
But I'm here to tell you I'm not part of a test.

I gave you everything I had
but that wasn't enough for you
because I know
you were never true.
And now you say
after going astray
that you've found yourself.
And it's for sure
you love me more
than ever before.

Well, you needn't humble yourself.
Because the love I had for you
has faded away.
You can't play with my heart
like it's a toy
you immature little boy.

No, you can't come back.
It's over now.
No, you can't come back.
You broke my heart
but I'm through crying.
I'm putting the pieces back together
and I'm going to give my love to someone else.

You Had It All, Lover

We met by chance
when I was so close
to giving up on love.
You made me smile and feel emotions
that I had never felt before.
You seemed to feel the same way.
We said, "no games, no lies."
It was love.
We had so much to give each other.
I would wake up in the morning
thinking about you
and go to bed at night
with only you on my mind.
Our erotic love was in another dimension.
Touching you in any way was ecstasy.
Our spiritual love was so strong,
it had to be everlasting.
We were the perfect couple.
No need would go unfulfilled.
We lived for each other.
No games, no lies.
Living for each other.
Then after a passionate night
of our bodies becoming one,
you tell me that you're married.
You had it all, lover
and I'm so close
to giving up on love.

Love Fantasy

I roam my fantasies
and dreams with you.
We love, we play,
we dance, and we cry.
But why do we cry
when we are so high
in ecstasy?

What more could we want?
What more could we ask?
Just the transition
from dream world
to real world.

There is always a full moon
and glittering stars to wish upon.
We wish for the same thing
every night,
and we know
that someday
it will come true.

Your life is spotlighted
in your eyes.
That life is my life.
Our hearts are one.
We were meant to be.
We were meant to be.

I know you so well.
But we haven't met.
And until we do
I will roam my
fantasies and dreams
with you.

You Touched My Soul

Like a magnet
we found each other
Nothing could keep us apart
Your handsome face
and strong body
is what I saw from the start
But nothing could compare
to what I was feeling
deep in my heart
Please don't be passing through
I already feel love for you
You know my needs
without me speaking
You're just the one
I've been seeking
No more barriers
No more baggage
My spirit is completely nude
Ready to go on an interlude
The doors are all open
so please come in
to a place no one
has ever been
Touch my soul
Touch my soul
Touch me.

Rainbow Love

Your love is like a rainbow
So beautiful
So colorful
So heavenly.
I never know
what to expect from you.
There are so many variations
of your love.
You keep me laughing and crying
happy tears.
Could it be that you were created in Loveland
by all the Gods of Love?
Just looking at you
makes me beam all over with pride.
Then I close my eyes and say
thank you for being who you are.

You're my king in a land
where royalty is admired.
I am your queen.
We serve each other.
Our kingdom is the rainbow love
that feeds our emotions and needs.

Thank you for being that rainbow
that appeared after all my rainy days.

You Gave Me Hope

Getting to know you
was such a pleasure

The happiness it brought
was too much to measure

You gave me hope
for a new life

I believed that one day soon
I would be your wife

The feelings were so strong
With you I could not go wrong

In you I saw the best
Waiting it out put me to the test

Your heart was so pure
And your love for me was so sure

I could call on you anytime
'cause your love was mine all mine

Impatience started to grow
But this relationship I will not blow

Because I know it won't be long
before they will be singing our song

A song of hope
for love and happiness

I've never known
anything better than this

We will come together
and unite our souls as one

And it's for sure
the fun has just begun

You gave me hope
for a new life

And it's all for real
because now I am your wife.

Yes, I'm Ready

Basics

You ask me what do I want
What do I look for in a man

Just the basics
Oh! You're not clear on what that is?

I want a man
who is honest as can be

with a personality
that makes him fun to be around

and a sense of humor
to turn a frown upside down

He's got to know what he wants
and go after it

With this kind of focus
he's got to be successful

And yes
he's got to know how to dress

Sexy scents are his
No drugs or cigarettes

Sharing true feelings
is very important to him

Because his goal is mutual happiness

Just the basics
That's all I want

Just the basics
That's what I have to give

Just the basics.

The Frame

Such a beautiful frame
But I don't need it
So I start to walk away
Such a beautiful frame
Heart shape and all
But my love has not arrived
So there is no face for it
Such a beautiful frame
I must have it
For the love that is to come
Even though I don't know his name
Such a beautiful frame.

Women And Men

I'm from Venus
He's from Mars
or so they say.
Why can't we form
our own planet,
starting today?
I will understand you,
you will understand me,
because we care
and we listen
with patience and sensitivity.

Us

You are my honey.
Being with you makes every day sunny.
When distance is between us
memories are truly a plus.
Although the relationship is young
the anthology of it should be sung.
For what we have
is not based on time
but what is truly in our hearts.
The closeness that we share lights the sparks
to a potion that is sweeter than wine.

Take My Hand

Take my hand.
I give you all of me.
Take my hand
and feel my presence with you
all the time.
You'll always have a friend.
You'll always have a lover.
You'll always have me.
Take my hand.

Progression

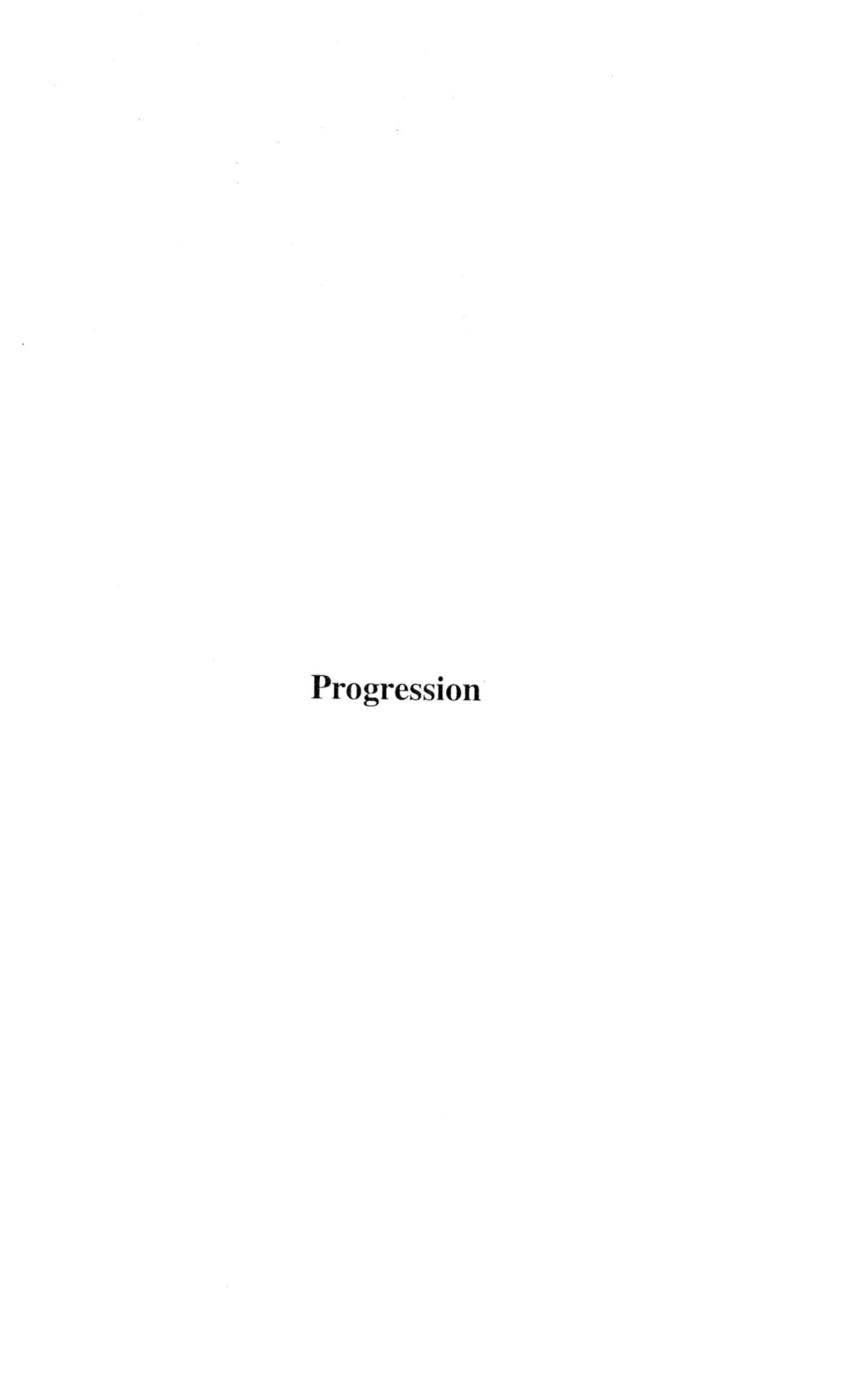

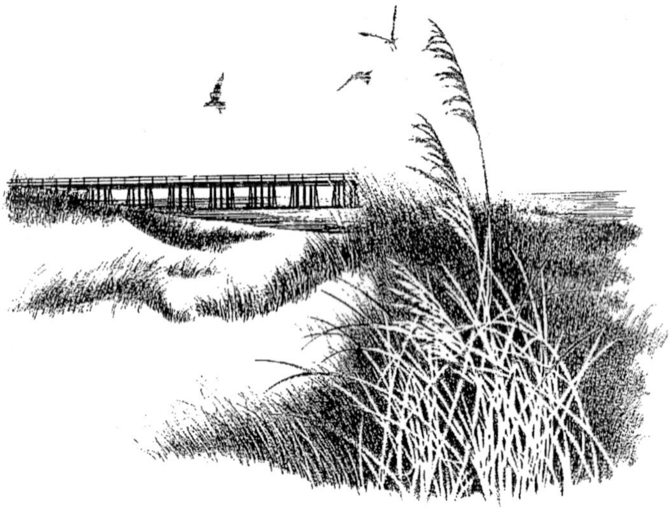

Sea Of Tranquility

When I feel stressed
I go to the sea
to get some tranquility.
The water helps me heal
and then I start to feel
a calmness come over me.
I wish I could stay
because I need this everyday.
But life calls me back
to its complexities.
So I will store this peace
in my spirit today
and let it guide me
on my journey all the way.

Hiding

Let's stop hiding
our true feelings,
our flaws,
our insecurities.
Get rid of
the layers of camouflage
that are barriers
to happiness.
Throw away the baggage.
Learn from mistakes.
And show the world
who you really are
by being that person.

Flaunt It

Flaunt it if you've got it.
Don't hold back.
Show the world you love yourself
and that it's not an act.

You have got the power within
to do what you want to do.
Let the greatness come out of you
to share with the world.

Flaunt it if you've got it.
Don't hold back.
You show pride in what you've got
and I like that.

It's no wonder
that your admirers
are dedicated to you.
They know that your personality
is so true.

Flaunt it if you've got it.
Don't hold back.

Mellowing

The Roses

You only gave me six.
I wanted twelve.
Why couldn't you do it right,
I thought again and again.
Questions came into my mind
because you didn't go all out.
I seemed to dissect everything
as if I wanted out.
The roses didn't look very fresh.
I thought they might go limp
in a day or two.
All of this translated
into the way I responded to you.
But your sincerity stood up
and stood out.
And nothing I said or did
could alter your heart
or diminish the gift
that blossomed into the
most beautiful six roses
that lasted longer than
any others
because they came with love.
And now our relationship
is growing with the nurturing.
Whether you give me one, six, or twelve,
Thank You!

Joy

I'm in such a good place
in every sense of the word.
The joy in my heart
shows on my face.
The flowers and trees
the water and sky
the mountainous earth
are the most beautiful
pieces of artwork.
Oh! What a joy
to feel such love
when I gaze upon
these ultimate creations.
Oh! What a joy.

Stop And Smell The Roses

From rags to riches
was the avenue I traveled.
Determination to have it all
kept me going.

The struggle was hard
but I had talent
and I knew it.

Success found me
ready, willing, and able
and it took me over.
I made it big, so big,
I could hardly believe it.

Then something went wrong.
I started falling, falling hard.
I soon realized
I never stopped
to smell the roses.

No one can climb
the ladder of success
unless they stop
to smell the
sweetness of life.

Otherwise, the bitterness
of it all will get the best of you.

I'm going to climb again
up that complex ladder.
And this time
I'll be able
to stay on top
because I'll be stopping,
stopping to smell the roses.

I Have The Power

I have the power
to make my dreams come true.
Life is too beautiful
for me to be blue.
Whatever brings me fulfillment
I must seek it,
knowing in my heart
that the rewards
will bring me contentment.
I have the power to be happy.
So my travels must be
on avenues that lead
to that destination.
And as I progress
I will spread the word
in ways to ensure
that my voice is heard.
I have the power.

Food For Thought

The Rain

Looking at the rain
is like looking at tears
from a world
that needs to be cleansed
of its sins.
Hatred
Racism
Evilness
Pollution
Hypocrisy
Wake up world.
Look at the bigger picture.
There is a Judgement Day
in many forms.
Improve yourself
and let the rain cleanse
not just fall
with no improvement at all.

Sometimes I wonder...

Why some people run away from happiness?

Why some people are hypocrites?

Why some people choose leadership roles and they are incompetent in that area?

Why some people have a problem giving compliments?

Where our society is going?

What happened to the unity of the '70's?

What happened to some of my ex-boyfriends?

Why some people get so jealous when you buy a brand new red Mercedes?

NOTES